BEST STORY

I0483214

NIBHA KUMARI

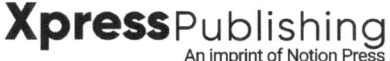

XpressPublishing
An imprint of Notion Press

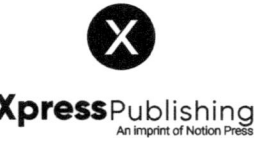

XpressPublishing
An imprint of Notion Press

Old No. 38, New No. 6
McNichols Road, Chetpet
Chennai - 600 031

First Published by Notion Press 2019
Copyright © Nibha Kumari 2019
All Rights Reserved.

ISBN 978-1-64678-839-2

Contents

Foreword

Hope you like it!

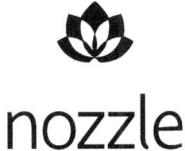

nozzle

Lighthearted short story on the request of colleagues ...

Nozzle

Zeenat was an athlete, representing the state level sports.

Seeing his better performance, a senior Indian administration official gave him his fellow

Chosen. Pair of Zeenat and Zaheer

The wedding was awesome

It was a year, they had to separate due to their busyness but the order of meeting twice a month

Sometimes it would break. Sometimes Zaheer used to come and sometimes Zeenat would be on her side.

Whenever they met, the world would get lost in the world. On a beautiful spring evening, both were in the restaurant. Zeenat was drinking coffee after dinner as usual. Zaheer was looking at her face while sipping coffee. Zeen's thick lashes

But the mascara had spread a little.

When Zaheer started cleaning her surplus mascara with her handkerchief, she started laughing profusely.

Zaheer used to take care of him like a child.

Zeenat was very beautiful, and had grown even more by getting such a noble husband. Her face was shababy and full of fun.

Here Zeenat had taken up a hobby. If she took anything for herself, matching the same color

The suit does not forget to take a shirt for Zaheer.

Zaheer seemed to have this extravagance, but would have kept quiet after seeing Zeenat's love.

He gave a long talk over the phone to make Valentine's Day memorable.

Zaheer said with great simplicity, "This time we will meet, I will take away the ATM card from you"

When did I ask for it? She said while shouting.

Zaheer always used to lose. This time too he kept quiet.

The talk has been made.

She leaves the airport, in front of Zaheer bouquet of fresh flowers

Jeet rose up from the light.

Zeenat had noor on his face. A few strands of loose hair were waving on his cheeks. Zaheer was lost in a pleasant mood.

Every word of husband meant for Zeenat. Later on

Thinking not to forget, he took out the ATM card from the purse and put it in Zaheer's pocket. He was oblivious.

Both of them kept talking on the beach for a long time. Zeenat started making gharaundas.

Zaheer bought gajera from a child selling gajra.

The evening started deepening. They were about to return home. They sat in the car. Suddenly Zaheer remembered something. He said "You have to book a ticket to return."

Get the card "

"I gave it to you at once. She was shocked.

When? He could not remember.

The pocket was searched and the card was missing.

Zaheer got upset. He started cursing when he

The card was handed over to Zeenat after being swept away in the emotions.

"Remember me properly". Zaheer started getting angry.

Zeenat was crying, the card was not visible on the purse.

Zeenat was saddened to find herself accused of negligence. A good mood was turned off for both of them.

The driver started the car. The car was about to turn towards the road, when the child selling the hawker

She came running. She had a card in her hand.

Actually, while withdrawing the money from Gajre, the card slipped and fell down, which the girl later saw and looking for it there.

she came.

He called the girl thank you and wanted to pay some money but the girl ran away laughing.

"Sorry" I did not realize. He smiled while pushing towards Gajra Zeenat.

"I don't want" that angry

She was angry and broke the gun

And started throwing flowers on Zaheer. The car had caught pace. The music system was on Lata ji's evergreen

The songs started buzzing.

Ho waking up. Smiling bouquet in front

Had been.

Swachit Nibha Kumari

CHAPTER TWO

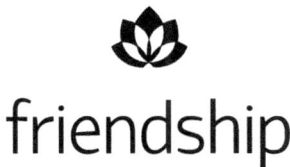

friendship

short story
 friendship
Shaheen Parveen and Kamala Bhattacharya were firm friends.
They both studied in school.
Hindus adjacent to school
Had houses. Everything was normal.
Fight some punks one day
In which a Hindu boy was badly injured.
This incident caught the color of communalism. Many houses were deliberately burnt by miscreants.
Shaheen got nervous when she was discharged in school. Kamala said "Shaheen Didi you are mine
Don't worry, let me show you
I leave home
Kakla shaheen leaving her
She went to the colony.
He crosses the raw street and inside
Was going
Then a woman with her
Six seven year old
The child was leaving his mother

Asked "Ammi, if all the people were Muslims then how good

Was not ".

The woman had her eye on Kamala. To silence the child

Was trying

Kamala finds something strange. Shaheen dares to leave the house

Full decision now for Kamala

Had become intimidating, as the incident was also being discussed there. While returning, saw that

Some people carried swords and throats in their hands. There was an atmosphere of warmth.

They hide their nervousness

"Someone" said to Akram Mian

What is the treat?

Old man scratching his long beard

Akram said "Adil's child has Sunna (a ritual)"

Kamala asked "When is good muhurta?

"We don't do any work by looking at the muhurta" he said carelessly.

All the answers to any danger

Began to warn.

Kamala leaves quickly

Wanted to go.

She increased. She started walking fast.

That's when Adil's voice was heard

Granted. "While I'm alive, you

But no heat will come.

Unperturbed vanity ".

Kamala arose and thanked the upstairs.

Moving on, a champagne smile blossomed on his face.

Swachit Nibha Kumari